The Marsupial Order

The Marsupial Order

REBECCA STEFOFF

 **Marshall Cavendish**
Benchmark
New York

*With thanks to Dan Wharton, Ph.D., Director, Central Park Zoo,
for his expert review of the manuscript.*

Marshall Cavendish Benchmark
99 White Plains Road
Tarrytown, New York 10591-9001
www.marshallcavendish.us
Text copyright © 2008 by Rebecca Stefoff
Illustrations copyright © 2008 by Marshall Cavendish Corporation
Illustrations on pages 16-17, 21, 25, 38, 40, 90-91 by Robert Romagnoli

All Web sites were available and accurate when this book was sent to press.

Editor: Karen Ang
Publisher: Michelle Bisson
Art Director: Anahid Hamparian
Series Designer: Patrice Sheridan

Library of Congress Cataloging-in-Publication Data
Stefoff, Rebecca, date
Marsupial order / by Rebecca Stefoff.
p. cm. -- (Family trees)
Summary: "Explores the habitats, life cycles, and other characteristics of organisms in the Marsupial Order"--Provided by publisher.
Includes bibliographical references and index.
ISBN 978-0-7614-2697-4
1. Marsupials--Juvenile literature. I. Title. II. Series.

QL737.M3S74 2007
599.2--dc22

Cover caption: A joey, or baby kangaroo, peeks out of its mother's pouch.
Back cover caption: A Tasmanian devil
Cover Photo: Frans Lanting / Minden Pictures
Photo research by Candlepants, Incorporated
The photographs in this book are used by permission and through the courtesy of: *ShutterStock:* 3, 6, 7, 19, 45, 47, 46, 56, 57, 65, 67, 82. *Corbis:* Stapleton Collection, 10; Academy of Natural Sciences of Philadelphia, 11; Louie Psihoyos, 20; DK Limited, 30; Theo Allofs/zefa, 34; Gary Bell/zefa, 35, 66; John Carnemolla, 48; Steve Kaufman, 53; Joe McDonald, 70; Michael & Patrcia Fogden, 72; Jose Luis Saavedra/Reuters, 77; Paul A. Souders, 87. *AP Images:* Tasmanian Department of Primary Industries, HO, 14 (top); Mark Duncan, 18; 33; The News Tribune, Janet Jensen, 86. *Getty Images:* Konrad Wothe, 22. *Photo Researchers Inc.:* Kenneth W. Fink, 14 (bottom), 79; 27; Dr. Eric Lindgren, 36; Martin Harvey, 41; William D. Bachman, 50; B. G. Thomson, 51, 60; Michael McCoy, 64; Gary Meszaros, 71. *Minden Pictures:* Norbert Wu, 29; Dave Watts/npl, 49, 62, 63; D. Parer & E. Parer-Cook/AUSCAPE, 52; Greg Harold/AUSCAPE, 54; Mike Gillam, 55; SA TEAM/Foto Natura, 69, 74; Cyril Ruoso\JH Editorial, 83. *Peter Arnold Inc.:* Doug Cheeseman, 31; Roland Seitre, 43; BIOS Cavignaux Régis, 44; Alain Compost, 61; S.J. Krasemann, 68; Luiz C. Marigo, 73; John Cancalosi, 81. *Animals Animals:* Dale & Marian Zimmerman, 75; Juergen & Christine Sohns, 78, back cover.

Printed in Malaysia

1 3 5 6 4 2

CONTENTS

Kangaroos were a mystery to the first Europeans who came to Australia. Nothing like these unusual creatures existed anywhere else.

Classifying Life

In 1606 a Dutch ship made the first European landing on an unknown coastline that lay south and east of Asia. That coast was the edge of a continent, a great southern island that would later be known as Australia. Several decades passed, and still only a handful of Europeans had laid eyes on Australia. Fewer still had set foot there. Then, in 1629, a Dutch ship called the *Batavia* was shipwrecked off Australia's western coast. The survivors were eventually rescued, and one of them, a man named Francisco Pelsaert, wrote the story of the wreck.

Pelsaert told of the tragic fate of the *Batavia*—a grim saga that included thievery and murder as well as shipwreck. But he also described some curious things the crew and passengers of the *Batavia* had seen in Australia. One of the oddest things was an animal that hopped about on two huge rear feet. Pelsaert did not know what to call this creature, which carried its newborn young in a fleshy pouch, or pocket, on the front of its body. The babies, Pelsaert wrote, were "only the size of a bean."

Pelsaert was the first European to describe a kangaroo. It's not surprising that he did not know what to call it. Nothing like this animal had ever been found in Europe, Africa, or mainland Asia. Europeans did know of some North and South American animals, the opossums, that carried their tiny young in pouches—but opossums did not hop like Pelsaert's animal. In an age before photographs, travelers' descriptions of kangaroos made people in Europe extremely curious about these unusual animals. When the first kangaroo was brought to England in 1791 and exhibited in a theater, mobs gathered to see it.

The kangaroo turned out to be just one of many pouched animals found only in Australia and nearby islands. These animals give birth to live young that are still at very early stages in their development. The young are then nurtured in their mothers' pouches until they are ready to come out into the world. All Australian and American animals with this kind of pouch are marsupials. Their name comes from *marsupium*, the Latin word for "pouch." To understand marsupials' place in the natural world, it helps to know something about how scientists classify living things.

THE INVENTION OF TAXONOMY

Science gives us tools for making sense of the natural world. One of the most powerful tools is classification, which means organizing things in a pattern according to their differences and similarities. Since ancient times, scientists who study living things have been developing a classification system for living things. This system is called taxonomy. Scientists use taxonomy to group together organisms that share features, setting them apart from other organisms with different features.

Taxonomy is hierarchical, which means that it is arranged in levels. The highest levels are categories that include many kinds of organisms. These large categories are divided into smaller categories, which in turn are divided into still smaller ones. The most basic category is the species, a single kind of organism.

The idea behind taxonomy is simple, but the world of living things is complex and full of surprises. Taxonomy is not a fixed pattern. It keeps changing to reflect new knowledge or ideas. Over time, scientists have developed rules for adjusting the pattern even when they disagree on the details.

One of the first taxonomists was the ancient Greek philosopher Aristotle (384-322 BCE), who investigated many branches of science, including biology. Aristotle arranged living things on a sort of ladder, or scale. At the bottom were those he considered lowest, or least developed, such as worms. Above them were things he considered higher, or more developed, such as fish, then birds, then mammals.

For centuries after Aristotle, taxonomy made little progress. People who studied nature tended to group organisms together by features that were easy to see, such as separating trees from grasses or birds from fish. However, they did not try to develop a system for classifying all life. Then, between 1682 and 1705, an English naturalist named John Ray published a plan of the living world that was designed to have a place for every species of plant and animal. Ray's system was hierarchical, with several levels of larger and smaller categories. It was the foundation of modern taxonomy.

Swedish naturalist Carolus Linnaeus (1707-1778) built on that foundation to create the taxonomic system used today. Linnaeus was chiefly interested in plants, but his system of classification included all living things. Its highest level of classification was the kingdom. To Linnaeus, everything belonged to either the plant kingdom or the animal kingdom. Each of these kingdoms was divided into a number of smaller categories called classes. Each class was divided into orders. Each order was divided into genera. Each genus (the singular form of genera) contained one or more species.

Linnaeus also developed another of Ray's ideas, a method for naming species. Before Linnaeus published his important work *System of Nature* in 1735, scientists had no recognized system for referring to plants and animals. Organisms were generally known by their common names, but many of them had different names in various countries. As a result, two naturalists

By the eighteenth century, scientists were eagerly studying marsupials. This early illustration of a koala shows the arrangement of toes that helps the animal cling to tree branches.

might call the same plant or animal by two different names—or use the same name for two different organisms. Linnaeus wanted to end such confusion, so that scholars everywhere could communicate clearly about plants and animals. He started the practice of giving each plant or animal a two-part scientific name made up of its genus and species. These names were in Latin, the scientific language of Linnaeus's day. For example, the long-tailed, tree-climbing marsupial known to Americans as an opossum has the scientific name *Didelphis virginiana* (or *D. virginiana* after the first time the full name is used). The genus *Didelphis* contains four kinds of opossums that live in the Americas. The single species that is native to the United States and Canada is set apart from the other three by the second part of its name, *virginiana*.

Linnaeus named hundreds of species. Other scientists quickly adopted his highly flexible system to name many more. The Linnaean system appeared at a time when European naturalists were exploring the rest of

John James Audubon, a famous nineteenth-century American wildlife artist, painted these Virginia opossums.

the world and finding thousands of new plants and animals. This flood of discoveries was overwhelming at times, but Linnaean taxonomy helped scientists identify and organize their finds.

TAXONOMY TODAY

Biologists still use the system of scientific naming that Linnaeus developed (anyone who discovers a new species can choose its scientific name, which

What's a Wombat?

Wombats are plump, clever, grass-eating, burrow-digging marsupials that live in Australia. The classification of one type of wombat shows how taxonomy moves from large categories to smaller and smaller ones.

In this traditional system of classification, the marsupials are an order. Other systems, however, place the marsupials—called the metatheria by some scientists—at the level of a subclass, infraclass, or superorder. Either way, the category of marsupials falls within the larger category of mammals that bear live young.

Kingdom	Animalia (animals)
Phylum	Chordata (animals with spinal cords)
Subphylum	Vertebrata (animals with spinal cords and with segmented spines)
Superclass	Tetrapoda (amphibians, reptiles, birds, and mammals)
Class	Mammalia (mammals)
Subclass	Theria (mammals that give birth to live young)
Order	Marsupalia—sometimes called Metatheria (mammals whose young develop in pouches after birth)
Suborder	Diprotodontia (marsupials with two incisor teeth in the lower jaw and two toes fused together on each foot)
Superfamily	Vombatoidea (wombats and koalas)
Family	Vombatidae (wombats)
Genus	*Lasiorhinus* (two species of hairy-nosed wombats)
Species	*latifrons* (southern hairy-nosed wombat)

is usually in Latin, or once in a while in Greek). Other aspects of taxonomy, though, have changed since Linnaeus's time.

Over the years, as biologists learned more about the similarities and differences among living things, they added new levels to taxonomy. Eventually, an organism's full classification could include the following taxonomic levels: kingdom, subkingdom, phylum (some biologists use division instead of phylum for plants and fungi), subphylum, superclass, class, subclass, infraclass, order, superfamily, family, genus, species, and subspecies or variety.

Another change concerned the kinds of information that scientists use to classify organisms. The earliest naturalists used obvious physical features, such as the differences between ducks and turtles, to divide organisms into groups. By the time of Ray and Linnaeus, naturalists could study speci-mens in more detail. Aided by new tools such as the microscope, they explored the inner structures of plants and animals. For a long time after Linnaeus, classification was based mainly on details of anatomy, or physical structure, although scientists also looked at how an organism reproduced and how and where it lived.

Today, biologists can peer more deeply into an organism's inner work-ings than Aristotle or Linnaeus ever dreamed possible. They can look inside its individual cells and study the arrangement of DNA that makes up its genetic blueprint. Genetic information is key to modern classifica-tion because DNA is more than an organism's blueprint—it also reveals how closely the organism is related to other species and how long ago those species separated during the process of evolution.

In recent years, many biologists have pointed out that the Linnaean sys-tem is a patchwork of old and new ideas. It doesn't clearly reflect the latest knowledge about the evolutionary links among organisms both living and extinct. Some scientists now call for a new approach to taxonomy, one that is based entirely on evolutionary relationships. One of the most useful new approaches is called phylogenetics, the study of organisms' evolutionary histories. Using a set of organizing steps called cladistics, scientists group

The black and white Tasmanian devil and the big-eared, big-footed red kangaroo may look quite different, but they share the basic features of the marsupial order.

together all organisms that are descended from the same ancestor. The result is branching, treelike diagrams called cladograms. These cladograms show the order in which groups of plants or animals split off from their shared ancestors.

Although none of the proposed new systems of classifying living things has been accepted by all scientists, the move toward a phylogenetic approach is under way. Most experts recognize the importance of cladistics while still using the two main features of Linnaean taxonomy: the hierarchy of categories and the two-part species name. Still, scientists may disagree about the proper term for a category, or about how to classify a particular plant or animal. Because scientists create and use classifications for many different purposes, there is no single "right" way to classify organisms.

Even at the highest level of classification, scientists take different approaches to taxonomy. A few of them still divide all life into two kingdoms, plants and animals. At the other extreme are scientists who divide life into thirteen or more kingdoms. Some now group the kingdoms into larger categories called domains or superkingdoms. Most scientists, though, use classification systems with five to seven kingdoms: plants, animals, fungi, and several kingdoms of microscopic organisms such as bacteria, amoebas, and algae.

The classification of living things is always changing, as scientists learn more about the connections among organisms. Although fossils prove that marsupials have been around for many millions of years, scientists are making new discoveries about these mammals. Meanwhile, the kangaroo has become a symbol of Australia. It appears on the nation's coat of arms and is instantly recognized around the world. People everywhere are also fascinated by chubby, teddy-bear-like koalas and by ornery Tasmanian devils. But there are more than three hundred kinds of marsupials in the world. All of them are remarkable, and some of them are in desperate need of protection.

Scientists classify living things in arrangements like this family tree of the animal

ANIMAL

PHYLA

CNIDARIANS

Coral

ARTHROPODS

(Animals with
external skeletons
and
jointed limbs)

MOLLUSKS

Octopus

**SUB
PHYLA**

CLASSES

CRUSTACEANS

Lobster

ARACHNIDS

Spider

INSECTS

Butterfly

MYRIAPODS

Centipede

ORDERS

CARNIVORES

Bear

SEA MAMMALS
(2 ORDERS)

Dolphin

PRIMATES

Monkey

16

kingdom to highlight the connections and the differences among the many forms of life.

KINGDOM

ANNELIDS

Earthworm

CHORDATES

(Animals
with a
dorsal
nerve chord)

ECHINODERMS

Starfish

VERTEBRATES

(Animals
with a
backbone)

FISH

Fish

BIRDS

Penguin

MAMMALS

AMPHIBIANS

Frog

REPTILES

Snake

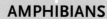

HERBIVORES
(5 ORDERS)

Horse

RODENTS

Squirrel

INSECTIVORES

Hedgehog

MARSUPIALS

Kangaroo

SMALL MAMMALS
(SEVERAL ORDERS)

Rabbit

The first mammals may have been small, tree-dwelling creatures similar to this tree kangaroo and her infant. These rare marsupials live in the forests of New Guinea, a large island north of Australia.

The Origins of Pouched Mammals

Why does Australia have more than two hundred kinds of marsupials, when most other parts of the world have none? The answer to that question became clear in the twentieth century, when scientists discovered how dramatically Earth's surface has changed over the past 250 million years. The slow but steady movement of Earth's continents shaped the history of the marsupials.

A large variety of marsupials—some of them giants—once roamed the ancient continents. Most became extinct. Yet the living marsupials are evidence of a great split that occurred long ago in the evolution of mammals.

MAMMALS AND MARSUPIALS

The ancestors of mammals were the therapsids, a large and long-lasting group of early reptiles. Over time, certain therapsids became more and more mammal-like, until by 220 million years ago, the first true mammals had appeared. They were small creatures, similar to today's shrews and opossums. And like shrews and opossums, they probably lived on a

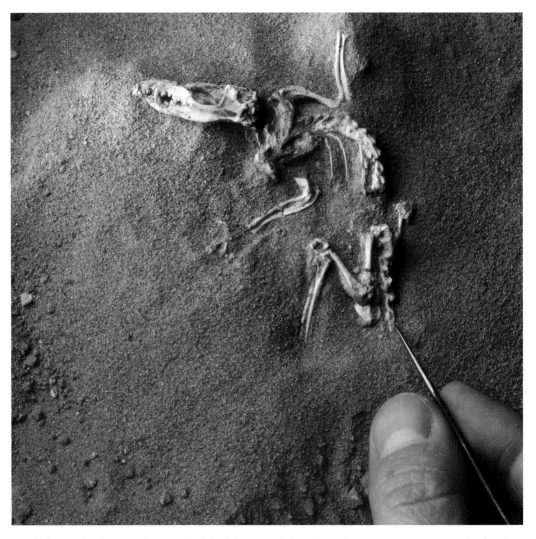

Barely five inches long, with a muzzle full of sharp teeth that show that it was a meat-eater, this fossil found in the Gobi Desert is all that remains of an early mammal that lived alongside the dinosaurs.

diet of insects, worms, and other small animals, although they may have eaten plants, too.

A combination of features set mammals apart from other animals. Mammals had hair for insulation. Their jaw was a single bone, while the jaws of other animals were made up of several bones. Mammals also had a set of small bones in their ears that gave them sharper hearing. But their most distinctive new feature of mammals was the mammae, or mammary glands. These glands are the source of our word "mammals." Feeding the young with milk from the mother's mammary glands is the defining feature of a mammal.

The therapsids gave birth to their young by laying eggs, and so did the early mammals. Some time after the evolution of the first mammals, a split took place in the mammal class. Some mammals continued to lay eggs. The rest began giving birth to live young. Today the egg-laying mammals form

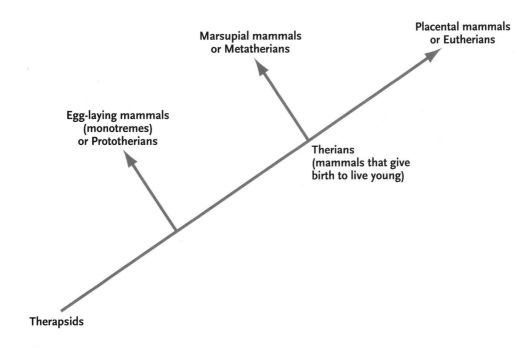

Scientists think that mammals evolved from a group of early reptiles called therapsids. Mammals then split into two groups: those that lay eggs, and those that bear live young. Later another division among the therians, or live-bearing mammals, led to the marsupials and the placental mammals.

one subclass of mammals. Traditionally they have been known as the monotremes, but some scientists use the name prototherians. The live-bearing mammals form a separate subclass, the therians. Scientists don't know for certain when the split between the monotremes and the therians took place. Most believe it happened at least 150 million years ago.

Another big split happened when one group of the live-bearing mammals branched off to become the marsupials, or metatherians. The remaining mammals—those that were neither monotremes nor marsupials—evolved into the placental mammals, or eutherians. Both groups bear live young, but marsupial newborns are very different from placental newborns.

Marsupials are born at an early, incomplete stage of their development. The time they spend developing inside the mother's body is fairly

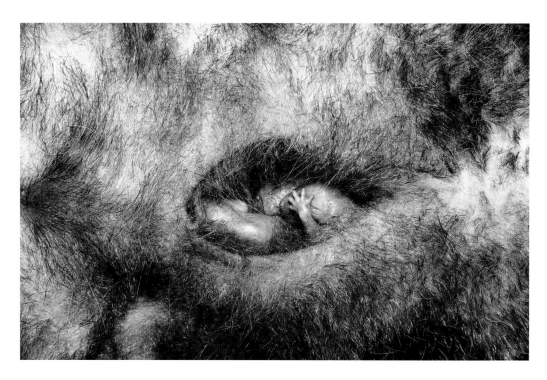

Born in an undeveloped state, the tiny newborn Virginia opossum will spend three months nursing in its mother's pouch before it is ready to come out into the world.

short—ranging from 9 to 42 days—and when they are born they are extremely tiny. In most cases, a litter of newborn marsupials weighs less than 1 percent of the mother's body weight. The hearts of newborn marsupials are not yet separated into chambers, and their eyes and ears are not yet formed. Their legs are mere buds. But their forelimbs are more fully developed, with paws that can grasp and climb, because the one thing a newborn marsupial must do is clutch its mother's fur and pull itself into the safety of her pouch.

Placental mammals give birth to newborns that are much more developed. The young have already spent a significant amount of time developing inside their mother's body. This period is called gestation. Early in gestation, eutherian embryos develop an organ called the placenta, which is attached to the mother's uterus and also attached to the embryo by the umbilical cord. Blood vessels in the placenta absorb oxygen and nourishment from the mother's body, for use by the young animal as it develops. When the young of eutherian mammals are born, newborns of some species need considerable care from their parents—human infants, for example, cannot move about or find food on their own for some time. Yet other eutherian young, such as newborn horses and elephants, can walk very soon after birth. In general, a placental newborn is physically complete and simply needs to grow.

The marsupials' method of giving birth to their young at an extremely early stage of development has one big advantage. It is easy on the mother. Pregnancy is short. A mother marsupial does not have to carry and feed the young inside her body during a long gestation. There is little risk to the mother's health in giving birth to such tiny young. If a marsupial becomes pregnant or gives birth during a bad season—when food is scarce, for example—she may lose her litter, but she will not have sacrificed a large investment of energy in them.

The marsupial method has some disadvantages, however. The tiny newborns are highly vulnerable to disease or accident. They are also born in what scientists call an altricial state, which means that they are helpless. They require a long period of care, and therefore a high investment of the mother's energy resources, after they are born. In addition, some biologists think that early birth may have limited marsupials' evolutionary possibilities. Among placental mammals, some lines of evolution led to animals with hoofs, wings, and flippers, but marsupials' front limbs always develop in the same way, because their grasping paws are vital to survival.

DRIFTING CONTINENTS AND DEAD DINOSAURS

Marsupials and placental mammals evolved around the same time. They separated from their shared ancestral line at least 125 million years ago. Based on measurements of the genetic distance between living species of marsupials and placental mammals, some researchers think that the split took place millions of years earlier. As for where it happened, people used to believe that marsupials originated in Australia, which has more marsupial species than anywhere else on earth. Many experts today, though, think that marsupials and placental mammals evolved in a place that no longer exists—a great landmass called Laurasia.

A big scientific breakthrough of the twentieth century was discovering that the earth's surface is constantly changing. The continents are huge plates floating on the melted rock that lies deep beneath the land and the seabed. These plates are in constant motion. They move a couple of inches a year, much too slowly for the movement to be seen in a human lifetime. But over vast spans of time their slow drift redraws the map of the earth's surface. Much remains to be learned about continental movement and about the evolution of marsupials, but for now the story goes like this:

When the ancestral marsupials and placental mammals began to evolve separately, all of the continental plates were jammed together into a single huge supercontinent. That enormous landmass is sometimes

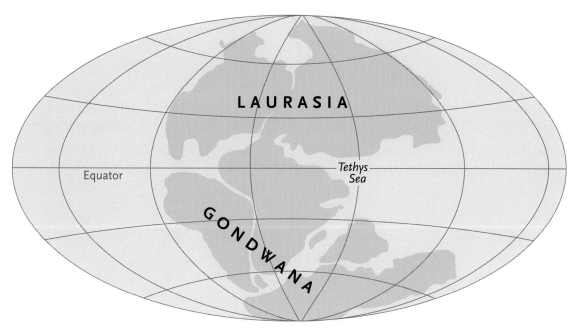

All of the present-day continents were once united in a single huge supercontinent that scientists call Pangaea. By 200 million years ago, Pangaea had split into Laurasia and Gondwana. They slowly drifted apart and broke up into smaller continents. Marsupials evolved in Laurasia but migrated into Gondwana before the landmasses separated. Later they died out in the northern continents that formed from Laurasia, but they continued to evolve in the southern continents that formed from Gondwana.

called Pangaea. Around 120 million years ago, Pangaea started to break up into two smaller landmasses. The northern landmass, which scientists call Laurasia, contained Asia, Europe, Greenland, and North America. The southern landmass, Gondwana, consisted of Africa, South America, Antarctica, Australia, and India.

Paleontologists, scientists who study fossils and other traces of ancient life, have found many bones of early marsupials in North America. One of the most ancient is a 100-million-year-old fossil found in Utah. In 2003, however, scientists reported finding an even older marsupial-like fossil in China. Named *Sinodelphys szalayi*, it is 125 million years old. Its skull, skeleton, and even traces of its fur were preserved. From the structure of its feet, scientists think that *Sinodelphys* was a good climber and might have been arboreal, or tree-dwelling. This find supports the idea that marsupials originated in Laurasia. But other ancient marsupial fossils have been unearthed in South America and the African island of Madagascar, and new discoveries may change our picture of marsupial origins.

Before Laurasia and Gondwana separated, some marsupials migrated south into Gondwana. Many marsupial families evolved in what is now South America. From there they spread into the regions that would become Antarctica and Australia. Then Gondwana itself broke up into separate continents. The various populations of marsupials kept on evolving, isolated from one another. Eventually Antarctica drifted into the cold south polar region, and its marsupials died out.

All this time, dinosaurs were the dominant land animals. Then, around 65 million years ago, the dinosaurs became extinct. Marsupials and placental mammals remained, and the disappearance of the dinosaurs let these small creatures move into habitats and ecological roles that had once been filled by dinosaurs. Metatherians and eutherians evolved rapidly into many new forms, some of them large. There were carnivores, herbivores, insectivores, and omnivores, mammals who ate both animal and plant foods.

Eventually, the marsupials that had lived in North America, Europe, Asia, and Africa followed the dinosaurs into extinction. It didn't happen overnight. North American marsupials survived until 15 to 20 million years ago. But it seems that the placental mammals were more successful than the marsupials at making use of resources, or better adapted to conditions. At any rate, eutherians flourished across the northern hemisphere while marsupials died out. In South America and Australia, though, marsupials survived.

THE GOLDEN AGE OF MARSUPIALS

For millions of years, South America was isolated from the other continents. Its plant and animal life evolved into a rich diversity of forms. A wide

Look-alike fossil skulls reveal that the marsupial *Thylacosmilus* (top) and the placental saber-toothed cat (bottom) had similar ways of life. Both were large, catlike predators. A favorite hunting technique was to pierce the prey's spine with the long, curved fangs.

range of mammals, including marsupials, roamed the land. Many of the marsupials were opossums, small to medium-sized long-tailed animals that were at home on the ground or in trees. Another group, the borhyaenids, were carnivores that looked something like present-day otters or wolverines, but bigger. Some borhyaenids were 6 feet (1.8 meters) long. They flourished during the Miocene Period, between 23 million and 5 million years ago.

The fiercest South American marsupial of the Miocene Period was probably *Thylacosmilus*, a large catlike predator. Its powerful shoulder, neck, and jaw muscles helped it grip and bring down large prey. *Thylacosmilus* also had a pair of long, curved fangs. It was very similar to the saber-toothed cats, placental carnivores that evolved in North America. This is an example of what biologists call convergent evolution—two unrelated groups of animals evolving in similar ways because they occupy similar habitats and adapt to similar lifestyles. *Thylacosmilus* looked a lot like the true saber-toothed cats, but it got that way through convergent evolution, not by being related to them.

In South America, marsupial and placental mammals evolved side by side. The two kinds of mammals remained in balance until about 3 million years ago, when sea levels around the world fell. The falling sea revealed a land bridge between South and North America. (Today that land bridge is called Central America.) A wave of new placental mammals traveled from North America to South America across this land bridge. Among them were predators such as bears, cats, and raccoons.

Soon after the North American newcomers arrived in South America, the golden age of South American marsupials came to an end. Most marsupials became extinct. The borhyaenids, *Thylacosmilus* and its relatives, and other large carnivores disappeared. Only the opossums survived. Some opossums even migrated northward and established themselves in Central America and southern Mexico. One species, *Didelphis virginiana* or the Virginia opossum, went all the way to North America. It became the only marsupial to live in North America since the extinctions of 15 million years ago or so.

Australia's marsupials were luckier. Their continent had separated from South America before many placental mammals reached it. Australian metatherians continued to develop without competition from eutherians. They also spread to the nearby large islands of New Guinea and Tasmania, and to some other islands as well, when periods of low sea level created land bridges that connected those islands to Australia and to each other.

The Australian marsupials developed into an even greater diversity of forms than the South American marsupials. Many families were herbivores, plant-eaters who ate fruit, browsed on leaves, or grazed on grass. One large group of mostly plant-eating marsupials, the diprodonts, evolved into several families. Among these were the possums (these animals are not the same as the American opossums), the koalas, and the wombats.

By 10 million years ago, another distinctive group of herbivores had evolved. These were the kangaroos, which moved like no other mammal: by hopping. Some researchers think that kangaroos evolved from a group of small, possumlike arboreal marsupials. As the climate grew drier, forests

A kangaroo mob—that's the correct term for groups of these animals—grazes in a landscape similar to the grasslands where their ancestors evolved.

gave way to plains across much of Australia. Animals came down from the trees and moved out into the grasslands. Over time, they adapted to new conditions by becoming larger and developing big feet and strong hind legs. They could stand on their hind limbs to see over tall grasses, and they could leap and bound forward at high speed to escape from predators. Herds of kangaroos filled the same ecological role that is filled by other grazing animals, such as wildebeests in Africa and bison in North America.

During the Pleistocene Epoch, between about 2 million years ago and 10,000 years ago, Australia was home to some enormous marsupials. The giant short-faced kangaroo, *Procoptodon goliah*, was the biggest kangaroo

The world's largest marsupial, *Diprotodon*, has been extinct for thousands of years. Its closest living relatives are the wombats and the koala. *Diprotodon* means "two forward teeth"—the two large teeth at the front of the upper jaw.

that ever lived. It stood more than 10 feet (3 m) tall and weighed 650 pounds (300 kilograms). Australia's biggest Pleistocene carnivore, *Thylacoleo carnifex,* has been called a marsupial lion. It was strong enough to prey on large kangaroos and haul them up into trees to eat them. The biggest marsupial of all, though, was a browsing herbivore called *Diprotodon optatum.* It was the size and shape of a modern hippopotamus or rhinoceros.

Nearly all of Australia's large animals became extinct at the end of the Pleistocene, between 10,000 and 20,000 years ago. The same thing happened on other continents, too. Scientists are not sure why, but there are several possible explanations. The world's climate had passed through many rapid changes as ice sheets repeatedly formed at the poles, then melted. Australia's climate had become cooler and drier, causing deserts to spread through the center of the continent and glaciers to form on the highest mountains. Some marsupials adapted to these changes, but many did not.

Humans might have played a part, too. The Aborigines, Australia's native inhabitants, arrived on the continent by at least 40,000 years ago, perhaps earlier. Some researchers believe that human populations, with their well-developed hunting skills, brought an end to the era of Australia's massive marsupials. The species that survived the Pleistocene extinction, along with those in the Americas, are the marsupials of the modern world.

An illustration of a thylacine—better known as a Tasmanian tiger or wolf—decorates a rock wall in Australia's Kakadu National Park. The rock art was created by the Aborigines, Australia's native people.

The Egg-Laying Mammals

The duck-billed platypus and the echidna, or spiny anteater, live in Australia and New Guinea, home of the majority of modern marsupials. They are not marsupials, though. They're something even rarer. They're monotremes.

Monotremes are mammals. They have fur and they suckle their young with milk from mammary glands. But monotremes do something no other mammals do—they lay eggs. Their eggs are enclosed in leathery shells, like reptile eggs. Monotremes resemble reptiles in other ways, too. For example, the structure of their hip and leg bones is more like that of reptiles than that of other mammals.

Scientists once thought that monotremes were primitive animals, the ancestors of modern marsupials and placental mammals. That view has changed. Scientists now know that the surviving monotremes are the last representatives of a very ancient group of mammals, but monotremes did not give rise to the other mammals. Instead, monotremes—or prototheria, as they are sometimes called—are a side branch on the evolutionary tree. They split off from the main line of mammal evolution before that line divided into marsupials and placental mammals.

Many monotremes are now extinct, known only from fossils. Only two families exist today. One family contains a single species, *Ornithorhyncus anatinus*, the duck-billed platypus. This animal lives near streams and ponds. A good swimmer, it hunts on the bottom for worms and small animals. The other family, the echidnas, contains four species. These long-snouted, spiny creatures live in burrows and root around on the forest floor for worms and grubs.

Platypuses and echidnas usually lay one egg at a time, although sometimes there are two or three. They incubate their eggs to keep them warm, just as birds do, until the eggs hatch. Then the young monotremes, sometimes called puggles, are fed by their mothers for four or five months, until they are ready to begin hunting for themselves. People sometimes confuse the monotremes with marsupials. But although monotremes live in the same region as many marsupials, and even share a few marsupial features (echidnas keep their newly hatched young in small pouches), the two are separate orders of mammals.

Found in the rivers and lakes of eastern Australia, the duck-billed platypus is one of the few egg-laying mammals to survive into modern times. The platypus may look comical, but spines on the males' hind legs hold venom that can kill small animals.

A koala and her young nestle together for a nap high in the branches of a eucalyptus tree, where these marsupials spend most of their time.

Modern Marsupials

Marsupials are a minority within the mammal class. Of the 4,600 to 5,000 known species of mammals, only about 300 are marsupials. Yet they span a greater range of sizes than any other order of mammals. The largest living marsupial is the red kangaroo, *Macropus rufus.* The body of an adult male may measure 5.2 feet (1.6 m) in length—with another 4 feet (1.2 m) for the tail. Most adult male red kangaroos weigh about 121 pounds (55 kg), but a few have been known to reach 198 pounds (90 kg).

At the other end of the size scale are the planigales, little rodentlike creatures that have been called marsupial mice. The smallest, *Planigale ingrami,* lives in northern Australia. It weighs about 0.15 ounce (4.5 grams) and is 3.7 inches (95 millimeters) long, including its tail.

Marsupials are equally varied in their ways of life. Some are forest-dwellers that eat fruit, leaves, and insects. A few are such specialized eaters that they seek out one particular food. Koalas eat the leaves and bark of eucalyptus trees. Numbats feast on termites, although they will also eat ants. Other marsupials graze on grasslands. Still others are hunters. Some American opossums, for example, catch and eat small mammals, birds, and amphibians such as frogs. Depending upon the species, marsupials

A mouse-sized red-tailed phascogale (an Australian marsupial that is also called a wambenger) makes a meal of a gecko.

may be diurnal (active by day), crepuscular (active at dawn or evening), or nocturnal (active by night).

The environments of marsupials range from desert to tropical rain forest. These adaptable animals live in trees, on the ground, and underground in burrows. One type of marsupial, the South American yapok, is semi-aquatic, spending part of its life in the water. And although no marsupial can fly, several species are gliders. Flaps of skin between their legs act as sails to support these animals as they swoop gracefully down through the air from high branches.

CLASSIFYING MARSUPIALS

Some biologists are "lumpers." They tend to group animals together in a single species unless there are strong reasons not to. Others are "splitters," more willing to place animals in different species. A splitter might see two or even three species where a lumper sees one. Decisions about species are even harder to make when scientists have seen only a few specimens. This is the case with some rare marsupials. As a result, biologists have differing ideas about how many species of marsupials exist today. Their figures range from about 270 to more than 330. *Walker's Marsupials of the World*, a handbook updated in 2005, recognizes 303 species of living marsupials.

The marsupial order is divided into seven suborders (some taxonomists call them orders within the marsupial infraclass). Three of the marsupial suborders are found in the Americas. The other four suborders are native to Australasia, which is the region that includes Australia, New Guinea, and neighboring islands.

At times scientists find it useful to divide marsupials into two large groups based on geography. The American marsupials are called the Ameridelphia. The Australian marsupials are the Australidelphia. Despite all of these divisions, though, all marsupials have some things in common.

BIOLOGY AND BEHAVIOR

If you could compare the brains of marsupials with the brains of placental mammals that are the same size and live in the same environments, you would notice some differences. The marsupials' brains, in general, would be a bit smaller. Their surfaces would have fewer folds, and the folds would not be as deep as on the placental mammals' brains. In some ways, marsupial brains seem to be simpler than eutherian brains.

Does this mean that marsupials are less intelligent? Some people used to think so. Marsupials, they argued, don't have the same complex social groups and communications systems as eutherians. They must be more primitive and less intelligent. But in recent years, observations of wild marsupials have shown that their behavior is surprisingly complex. Marsupials, it is now known, have the ability to learn new things. The idea that they are inferior to eutherians is no longer part of scientific thinking.

MARSUPIAL SKULLS

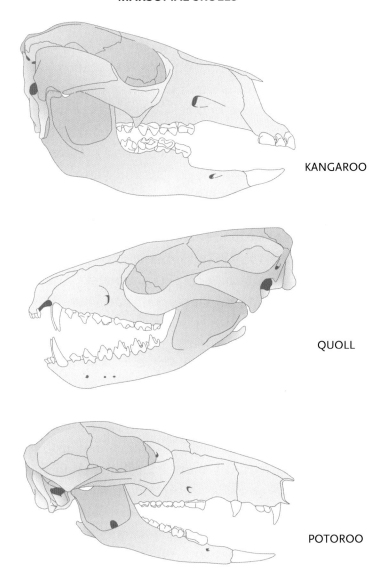

KANGAROO

QUOLL

POTOROO

Marsupials have different kinds of teeth, depending upon their lifestyles. The kangaroo browses on vegetation, with cutting teeth in front for chopping plants and flat molars on the sides for grinding them. The quoll, a marsupial "cat," is a carnivore, equipped with teeth for biting and tearing flesh. The potoroo is an omnivore that eats insects and other small prey as well as plants. It has sharp teeth for biting and flat molars for grinding vegetation.

Many researchers believe that there is much more to be learned about marsupial behavior. One area that scientists are now studying is how marsupials use smell and sound to communicate. Other biologists are investigating the way that some marsupials, including various kangaroo species, form social or family groups.

In spite of their great range of body sizes and shapes, marsupials share some physical characteristics. Some distinctive features are invisible to the ordinary viewer because they have to do with the animals' skeletons and teeth. Marsupials (and the egg-laying monotremes) have an epipubis, a bone that is attached to their pelvis. The epipubic bone may anchor muscles that support a male marsupial's sex organs. Another possibility is that muscles attached to the epipubic bone help support the animal's body while its legs are moving. Whatever the epipubic bone does, placental mammals do not have it. Another difference is that most placental mammals have an equal number of incisors, or front teeth, in their upper and lower jaws. Most marsupials, however, have more incisors in their upper jaws than in their lower jaws.

REPRODUCTION AND LIFE CYCLES

Marsupials have various patterns of courtship and mating. Quite a few marsupial species are solitary. Individual animals spend most of their time alone. Males and females come together only to mate, and they do not stay together afterward. In some species, both the male and female mate with multiple partners during each breeding season.

Male koalas can become ferocious when defending their breeding territories. Each territory is occupied by a single male and at least one female—some males try to include several females in their territories. The male mates with all of the available females in his territory and drives off any other males who try to mate with those females. Even when mating season is over, koalas are protective of their territories—which are not

RED KANGAROO SKELETON

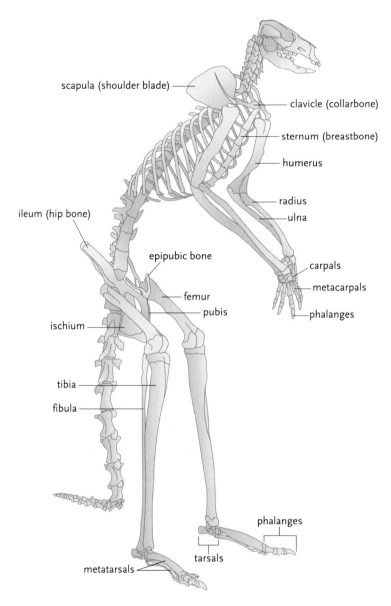

scapula (shoulder blade)

clavicle (collarbone)

sternum (breastbone)

humerus

radius

ulna

ileum (hip bone)

epipubic bone

carpals

metacarpals

femur

pubis

phalanges

ischium

tibia

fibula

phalanges

tarsals

metatarsals

The skeleton of a red kangaroo, the largest living species of marsupial, shows how the animal's anatomy is adapted for hopping, with long feet, strong leg bones, and a powerful tail that is long enough to reach the ground and act like an extra leg. The epipubic bone of the pelvis is a part of the skeleton found only in marsupial and egg-laying mammals.

large, usually consisting of just a few good-sized food trees. An intruder into a koala's territory is likely to meet with bellows, shrieks, and even attacks.

Kangaroos of some species live in large, organized groups called mobs. So do some wallabies, which are simply small kangaroos. The whiptail wallaby, *Macropus parryi*, may be the most social of all marsupials. It lives in mobs of thirty to fifty animals. Within each mob, the adult males form a hierarchy, or "pecking order," based on rank. They establish their rank by pawing each other in a show of strength. Although the wallabies don't

Natural kickboxers, kangaroos use all four limbs when they fight. Some fights are playful. Others are more serious, such as when males fight over females.

injure each other in these bouts, the larger males dominate the smaller ones. Only the males in the upper ranks of the hierarchy can mate with the females.

The greater gliding possum (*Petauroides volans*) follows a different mating arrangement. These arboreal marsupials of Australia's east coast woodlands form pairs. Some males pair with one female, others with two females who live separately. Males and females don't spend all their time together, but they interact throughout the year, not just at breeding season. The females, however, do all the infant care.

The life cycle of a marsupial begins when its parents mate. If the female becomes pregnant, the short gestation period is followed by birth—most of the time. In nearly all species of kangaroos and wallabies, and some species of possums, the female can put her pregnancy on hold. The embryo halts in its development at an extremely early stage. It remains in the female's reproductive organ, her uterus, until it receives a chemical signal to start developing again.

This delay in an embryo's development is called diapause. It can last for days, weeks, or even months. Diapause allows the female to mate and then postpone her pregnancy while she is still nursing her young from an earlier pregnancy. This is necessary because she cannot care for a newborn and a partly grown offspring at the same time. When she has stopped nursing the first offspring, her body releases the chemical that is the signal for the embryo's development to start up again. At that point the gestation period begins.

After the short marsupial gestation period, birth occurs. Because young marsupials are so tiny and fragile, they can be easily damaged, and birth can be dangerous for them. Female marsupials usually give birth while sitting on their tails with their bottoms tilted forward. When the young emerge from her body, they are close to her belly fur. They grasp it and wriggle toward her mammary glands, probably guided by their sense of smell. This journey is short, but it is the most important journey in a marsupial's life. The newborn red kangaroo, for example, must cover a

An infant red kangaroo, attached to the nipple in its mother's pouch, is 3 inches (8 cm) long. Its eyes have not yet developed.

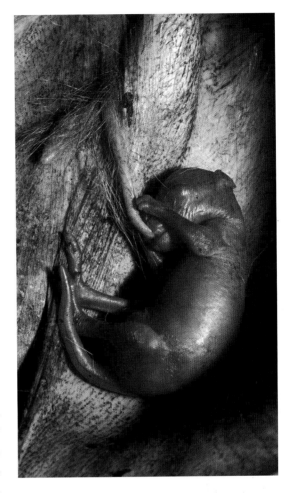

distance of only 6 or 7 inches (15.25 or 17.75 centimeters) to reach its mother's pouch and the mammary glands inside the pouch—but the newborn is very small and vulnerable. It takes this tiny, unfinished creature several minutes to "swim" upward with its forelegs to safety.

Once a newborn marsupial reaches its mother's mammary glands, it fastens itself to the nipple of one of the glands and starts receiving its mother's nourishing milk. The young will remain attached to the nipple until they are well enough developed to move around inside the pouch or to be left in nests while their mother forages for food. This can take anywhere from a month to more than three months, depending on the species.

Not all marsupials have pouches to hold their young. Only about half of all species are pouched, and in some of these species, the pouch forms only when the mother is breeding. In other species, including some opossums and the numbat, or spiny anteater, there is no true pouch, just protective folds of skin around the mammary glands. Either way, newborn marsupials spend the first stage of their lives fastened to their mothers' nipples. She carries them wherever she goes.

Even after a young marsupial is able to move around on its own, it depends on its mother for milk and protection. In species with pouches, this is the in-and-out period of life—the young spend part of their time in the pouch, with periods outside the pouch that become longer and longer. The young of other species may ride around on their mother's back, or under her belly, clinging to her fur, but they gradually become more and more independent. A little at a time, they start eating the same food their mother eats. When the young are able to live on solid food alone, the mother stops nursing them. This is called weaning.

By the age of six months, this young Bennett's or red-necked wallaby has developed most of its physical features, but it won't be ready to leave the pouch for another three months.

A young brush-tailed possum hitches a ride on its mother's back. These plant-eating, nocturnal possums are among Australia's most common marsupials.

Young marsupials that have been weaned may remain with their mother until she has new offspring that demand her attention, or they may drift off to live independently soon after weaning. They continue to grow until they have reached sexual maturity. This can take up to seven years in some kangaroo species, or as little as three months for some bandicoots. Once the marsupial is sexually mature, it is ready to mate and produce its own offspring. The cycle of life starts again at the beginning.

The wombat is the marsupial version of the groundhog or marmot. Wombats are sturdy diggers, with strong legs and long claws. They make burrows that they often share with other wombats.

The Marsupials of Australia

The world's greatest diversity of marsupials is found in Australia and its island neighbor to the north, New Guinea. Some of the Australian marsupials also live on other, smaller islands in the region. The seven suborders of Australian marsupials contain more than two hundred species. Koalas and kangaroos are well-known and popular. But how many people outside Australia have heard of marsupial cats and mice—not to mention bandicoots, cuscuses, quokkas, and bilbies?

CARNIVOROUS MARSUPIALS

Nearly all of Australia's meat-eating marsupials are grouped together in the suborder Dasyuromorphia. It is one of the larger marsupial suborders, with more than sixty known species. Two of the most famous species in the suborder are known only from the island of Tasmania, which lies off the southern coast of the Australian continent and is part of the nation of Australia.

One of those famous marsupials was the biggest marsupial carnivore of recent times, and the top predator of Tasmania. It was *Thylacine*

Hunted to extinction by European settlers, the Tasmanian tiger or wolf is now known only from stuffed specimens in museum exhibits.

cynocephalus, the thylacine—also called the Tasmanian tiger or Tasmanian wolf. This doglike marsupial, with black stripes on gray or yellow-brown fur, lived in Tasmania when Europeans began raising sheep on the island in the nineteenth century. Before long, the Europeans had decided that the thylacine was an unacceptable threat to their livestock. Rewarded by private and government bounties paid for dead thylacines, settlers killed thousands of the animals with guns, traps, and poison. The loss of the tigers' habitat to ranchland and competition from dogs and other animals introduced by the Europeans also hurt the thylacines. By 1914, thylacines had become very rare. The last known member of the species died in 1936. Today the Tasmanian tiger is officially considered extinct.

A smaller Tasmanian carnivore is not yet extinct. It is the Tasmanian devil, *Sarcophilus harrisii.* Devils once lived throughout much of mainland Australia, but they were gone when Europeans arrived. Some researchers

Tasmanian devils communicate with ear-splitting screeches, snarls, and squalls. Their powerful jaws chew through carcasses, eating the bones and fur as well as meat.

think that the mainland devils were driven into extinction by the Aborigines' dogs, the dingoes. Devils became scarce in Tasmania, too, in the early twentieth century, but their numbers later increased in some areas.

Researchers have found that devils are less harmful to healthy livestock than was once thought, and that they play an important ecological role as scavengers of roadkill and other dead animals. They have also learned that devils do not deserve their early reputation as savage monsters. After years of observing devils, wildlife filmmaker David Parer said, "We think of them as bad-tempered and vicious, but watch them in the den and their family lives are not unlike a human life. There's playtime, squabbles, dinner time, discipline problems, teaching and learning." Today many

Tasmanians proudly regard these sharp-toothed, scrappy marsupials—known for their noisy but often harmless brawls with each other—as symbols of their homeland. The devil is pictured in the official logo of the Tasmania Parks and Wildlife Service.

Another carnivore is the numbat, whose preferred prey is termites and ants. Numbats measure 69 to 108 inches (175 to 275 cm) in body length, with long furry tails. Numbats have no pouches. As with other pouchless marsupials, the young attach themselves to the mother's nipples, and she carries them around under her body. As the young get larger, they sometimes drag on the ground while their mother is carrying them. Good climbers, numbats are active by day, trotting about in search of termite nests in logs and soil. They tear into the nests with their sturdy front claws and scoop up the insects with their long, flexible tongues.

The suborder Dasyuromorphidae also includes a number of small, pointed-nosed, long-tailed species that are sometimes called marsupial

The numbat is most often seen on or near fallen trees. Numbats seek shelter in hollow logs, which also provide food for the termites that numbats eat. Unlike most marsupials, numbats are active by day.

mice. These marsupials are completely unrelated to true mice, which are placental mammals, but their appearance is somewhat similar. The marsupials in these genera are known by a wide variety of names: dunnarts, ningauis, phascogales, antechinuses, and more. They eat insects, worms, spiders, and possibly, in some cases, other small animals or birds. Some species have a tail that is adapted to store food. When the animals eat well in times of plenty, their tails swell with fat, becoming carrot-shaped. When food is scarce, the animals can live off the stored fat.

Just as there are marsupials called mice, there are also marsupial "cats." Known as tiger cats, native cats, or quolls, these half-dozen species are not really cats but marsupials that hunt for prey, usually by night. Their large eyes give them keen eyesight. They eat insects, smaller marsupials, and rodents. The largest quoll, *Dasyurus maculatus,* weighs 4.5 to 6.5 pounds

The mulgara, a mouse-sized marsupial predator, searches the tops of grasses for insects.

A female eastern quoll leads her young through the Tasmanian forest. Quolls are about the size of cats. They feed on small birds and animals, but their most common prey is insects.

(2 to 3 kg). It has become rare on the mainland but also lives in Tasmania. Two other species of quolls are found in New Guinea.

BANDICOOTS AND BILBIES

The suborder Peramelemorphia contains about 22 species of the pouched marsupials known as bandicoots. The largest are the rainforest bandicoots of New Guinea, members of the genus *Peroryctes,* which can have a tip-to-tip length of 35 inches (89 cm) and can weigh 10.3 pounds (4.7 kg). Most bandicoots, however, are considerably smaller. Some species, such as *Peroryctes raffrayana,* have soft, short, sleek fur. The New Guinea spiny

After spending its day in a nest—a shallow hole in the ground, covered with a mat of grass—the eastern barred bandicoot digs for worms, grubs, and beetles by night.

bandicoots, members of the genus *Echymipera*, have long, stiff, spiny fur. Bandicoots have many small teeth, and long, thin legs and tails. They have long noses—even the species known as short-nosed bandicoots. They also have large ears. In one group of species, the bilbies or rabbit-eared bandicoots, the ears are especially long and flexible. To sleep, bilbies rest on their hind legs, tuck their faces between their front paws, and fold their ears forward to cover their eyes.

Bandicoots have a special development of their feet that is called syndactyly. On their hind feet, the second and third toes are enclosed together inside a sheath of skin. Only the tops of these toes and their claws are separate. Bandicoots use the "combined" toe with two nails like a small comb for grooming their fur. The fourth toe is larger than the fifth toe,

The greater bilby once lived in most of Australia. Today it is limited to a few desert areas. Cats and foxes, introduced by European settlers, have wiped out bilbies in much of their former range.

while the first toe is tiny or altogether missing. On bandicoots' front feet, the first and fifth toes are usually small or missing. The other front toes are well developed and used for digging.

Bandicoots live in grassy nests and forage for food on the ground by night. Alert and quick-moving, they feed on insects and other animals as well as on fruits and other plant food. They are omnivores, animals that eat all kinds of food.

THE MARSUPIAL MOLE

The thylacine was an example of convergent evolution. It was a marsupial mammal that had evolved in such a way that it looked a lot like a dog or wolf, because its way of life and environment were much like those of dogs and wolves. Another striking example of convergent evolution is Australia's marsupial mole, *Notoryctes typhlops*.

Notoryctes isn't related to the placental moles, which are small burrowing, near-blind creatures that spend most of their lives underground. But it looks and acts a lot like them. Like moles, *Notoryctes* is covered with fine, soft fur. Its large, curved claws are perfect for digging and scooping dirt as it tunnels through sandy soil searching for insects, especially beetle larvae. (Unlike true moles, *Notoryctes* has a pouch for its young. The pouch opens to the rear so that it does not collect dirt.) Although *Notoryctes* has an optic nerve, its eyes have almost disappeared. They are tiny, hidden beneath its skin. The animal's snout is protected by a hard, hornlike shield.

Scientists debate whether marsupial moles are one species or two. Either way, they are the only animals in the suborder Notoryctemorphia.

In the Tanami Desert of Australia's Northern Territory, a marsupial mole devours a centipede.

Although these animals were once hunted for their pale, silky fur, habitat loss is now their biggest threat. They are considered endangered.

KOALAS, KANGAROOS, AND THEIR KIN

With about 130 species, the suborder Diprotodontia is larger than all the other suborders of Australian marsupials put together. This diverse suborder is made up of ten families. Among them are some very recognizable marsupials, such as koalas and kangaroos, as well as many that are less well known, such as possums and gliders.

The koala lives on eucalyptus leaves. That's a low-energy diet, but the koala's life does not demand a lot of energy. The animal spends up to twenty hours of each day asleep.

The koala, *Phascolarctos cinereus*, looks like a toy bear, but it is not related at all to true bears. It spends most of its time in eucalyptus trees, where it eats, sleeps, and raises its young. The koala's feet are well adapted to an arboreal life. On the front feet, the first and second toes are opposable to the other three, like a thumb on a human hand. This helps give the koala a good grip on branches. The first toe of each of its hind feet is also opposable, while the second and third toes are fused together, but with separate claws. Like bandicoots, koalas use these claws to comb their fur. Most diprotodonts—as members of the suborder Diprotodontia are called—have syndactylous feet.

Koalas live almost entirely on eucalyptus leaves and bark. Because leaves and bark are not very nutritious, koalas have to eat a lot of leaves to get enough nutrition. Their cheek pouches expand to store leaves. And although the koala's body is no longer than 33.5 inches (85 cm), a section of its intestine called the cecum can be as much as 8.25 feet (2.5 m) long. This long intestine is needed to digest the tough leaves.

Another family of diprotodontids contains Australia's three species of wombats: common, northern-hairy-nosed, and southern hairy-nosed. These stocky, strong, burrow-dwelling marsupials look something like small bears, or possibly the groundhogs and marmots of North America. They measure between 27.5 and 47 inches (70 and 120 cm) in length and weigh from 33 to 77 pounds (15 to 35 kg).

Wombats are generally slow-moving, but a wombat in a hurry can reach speeds of 25 miles (40 km) an hour, although only for a minute or two.

A Boy and His Wombat

Peter J. Nicholson was a teenager at boarding school in Australia in 1960, when one day he was told to report to the headmaster's office. Thinking, "Gosh, this sounds like trouble," Nicholson nervously went to the office. It turned out that all the headmaster wanted was for Nicholson to show some wombats to a science teacher.

The boy led the teacher out of the school to a nearby area of wombat burrows. Outside one burrow, Nicholson made a few wombat noises. A wombat that had gotten to know Nicholson came out and sniffed at the boy's feet, and that was the end of the evening's wombat expedition. But how had the wombat gotten to know Nicholson? That was the real adventure—and the reason Nicholson had been afraid he was in trouble.

Nicholson had been in the habit of sneaking out of his room at night and exploring the wombat burrows. Not just looking at them from outside, but crawling down into the tunnels, around twists and turns and through tight spots, risking death if the tunnels collapsed. He was the first person, as far as anyone knows, to enter the underground world of the wombat.

After growing up in the country—the bush, as Australians call it—Nicholson was interested in all animals. He found wombats especially easy to observe because they didn't run away as fast as kangaroos, or fly away like birds, or climb high up in the trees. They simply waddled into holes in the ground. "And by the time I'd stuck my head down to see what was in there," Nicholson said years later in an interview for the

Australian Broadcasting Corporation, "the temptation was to stick it a little bit further and to see whether there was anybody at home in these burrows. And I think that's how it started."

Over a period of months, the tall but skinny Nicholson explored a cluster of wombat burrows. He carried a flashlight so that he could see and a trowel for digging his way through tight places. With pegs and string he marked stretches of tunnel, measuring the string later so that he could map the forks and turns of each burrow. By going in as far as 70 feet, Nicholson came to understand the architecture of each burrow. Sometimes he went all the way to the wombat's nest at the end. He moved slowly, perhaps taking weeks to get to know a particular wombat, resting quietly in its burrow and copying its grunting sounds until it got used to his presence. That's how Nicholson was able to show "his" friendly, curious wombat to the visitor.

Nicholson used his secret adventures as the subject of a report on wombat burrows, complete with diagrams. It won first prize in a student science contest. More than that, for more than forty years scientists recognized Nicholson's schoolboy science paper as the best piece of research that had ever been done on wombat burrows. As for Nicholson, he grew up to become a businessman with a lasting admiration for wombats and other wildlife, as well as a deep commitment to protecting Australia's environment and natural wonders.

A brush-tailed possum jumps from one tree to another.

A family called the phalangerids contains about 22 species of possums and cuscuses. This family is very widespread. Members are found in Australia, Tasmania, New Guinea, and other islands from the Solomon Islands group in the east to the Indonesian island of Sulawesi (formerly Celebes) in the west. One species of brush-tailed possum, *Trichosaurus vulpecula,* lives in New Zealand. It was carried there in recent times by humans.

Possums and cuscuses tend to have thick, plushy fur. They have opposable toes, which make them good climbers, and most species are arboreal. Prehensile tails, which are flexible and can be used almost like extra limbs, contribute to their climbing ability. Possums have been seen dangling from branches by their tails while they eat a piece of fruit. The scaly-tailed possum, *Wyulda squamicaudata,* has a tail that is, as its common name suggests, covered with scales, except at the base where it is furry. All other members of this family of marsupials have furry tails. Most of them eat fruit, seeds, leaves, and grasses, although some also feed on insects, eggs, and young birds.

Five other families contain possums, too. One family consists of the genus *Acrobates,* which has two species: the feather-tailed possum of New Guinea and the feather-tailed glider of Australia. Long hairs on the sides of these marsupials' tails give the tails the appearance of feathers. The honey possum, *Tarsipes rostratus,* is the only species in its family. It lives in the southwestern part of the state Western Australia and lives on nectar and pollen. Small and nimble, the honey possum climbs from tree to tree to poke its long snout into flowers.

The petaurids, a family of gliding and striped possums, includes about 10 species. All of them are arboreal, and some of them almost never come down from the trees to the ground. Some of them glide, like the flying

The sugar glider, *Petaurus breviceps,* can sail through the air as far as 165 feet (50 m) after launching itself from high in a tree.

squirrels of North America, by spreading their limbs wide to open sail-like membranes between their front and hind legs. These species have common names such as sugar glider, squirrel glider, and fluffy glider.

The greater gliding possum, *Petauroides volans,* belongs to a different family, the family of ring-tailed possums. *P. volans* can sail over distances of up to 330 feet (100 m). It can alter its direction in the air, possibly by moving its long tail. The other six species of ring-tailed possums are not gliders, but they are good climbers that spend most of their lives in trees, eating leaves and fruit.

Pygmy possums are found in Australia, Tasmania, and New Guinea. Four of the species in this family are called dormouse possums because they look like small European animals known as dormice. They have plump bodies, soft fur, and large, almost hairless ears. Adult dormouse possums have a maximum body length of 4.7 inches (12 cm), although their tails are likely to be equally long. They live in trees and eat a wide variety of foods.

The fifth species in the pygmy possum family is *Burramys parvus,* the mountain pygmy possum. Scientists used to think this species had become extinct about 15,000 years ago. They had found fossils, but never live animals. Then, in 1966, an unknown possum turned up inside a ski hut in the mountains of the state of Victoria,

The little pygmy possum, also called the Tasmanian pgymy possum, is Australia's smallest possum. Its average body length is 2.5 inches (6.4 cm), and its tail is a bit longer than its body.

Australia. Many more mountain pygmy possums have been observed since that time. These animals live in mountains where they must survive harsh, snowy winters. They are the only marsupials known to collect and store foods such as seeds for later use. Mountain pygmy possums may also hibernate during the winter, entering a state similar to sleep that saves energy.

The potoroids are another family of diprotodonts. This family includes the three known species of potoroos (one of them has been considered likely extinct since the 1970s). Potoroos resemble miniature kangaroos. Like kangaroos, they sometimes walk slowly on all four legs and sometimes travel by hopping and bounding with the aid of large feet. The biggest potoroos are about 16 inches (41.5 cm) long and weigh 4.8 pounds (2.2 kg). The long-nosed potoroo, *Potorous tridactylus,* has been studied in some detail. Scientists discovered that it eats a lot of insects and fungi in addition to grasses and roots.

A long-footed potoroo scuttles across the forest floor on a nighttime hunt for insects.

Also included in the potoroid family are a variety of little marsupials called rat-kangaroos. Some of them, like potoroos, look and move a lot like small kangaroos. They have very long hind feet and short forelegs. Their habitats range from dense rain forests to grasslands to sandy semi-desert with only a few scattered bushes for vegetation. Some rat-kangaroos are burrowers. Others are nest-builders and have been sighted carrying nest materials, such as grass and sticks, by curling their prehensile tails around them.

Kangaroos and wallabies make up the macropods. With more than 60 species, this is the largest family in the diprotodont suborder. The macropods—the name means "big feet"—vary greatly in size. Red kangaroos and grey kangaroos can be bigger than an average-sized person, while small hare wallabies can weigh less than 1 pound (.45 kg).

The diverse macropod family includes the possum-like quokka, *Setonix brachyurus*, which weighs between 5 and 11 pounds (2 and 5 kg), and the pademelons, six species of small, kangaroo-like marsupials that resemble rabbits in their habit of thumping their feet on the ground to signal each other. There are also ten species of tree kangaroos, found in mountainous rain forests in New Guinea

Red-legged pademelons live in the rainforest of northern Australia but often venture into suburban backyards and parks to feast on fruit.

Yellow-footed rock wallabies peer out from their rocky refuge. Often found in hilly or mountainous areas, these wallabies can leap swiftly from rock to rock, like mountain goats.

and northern Australia. The tree kangaroos are the only macropods that don't move by hopping or bounding on their hind legs.

Hopping and bounding come quite naturally to the many species of kangaroos, wallaroos, and wallabies. Kangaroos are the largest species in this family. Some biologists now limit the name "kangaroo" to the three largest marsupial species: the red kangaroo (*Macropus rufus*), the eastern grey kangaroo (*Macropus giganteus*), and the western grey kangaroo (*Macropus fuliginosus*). Another three species of good-sized, shaggy-furred macropods are sometimes called wallaroos. The rest of the macropods are wallabies. They are usually smaller than kangaroos and wallaroos. The smallest is the parma wallaby (*Macropus parma*) of New South Wales in Australia. Adult parma wallabies average 18 inches (47 cm) or so in body length, with tails of about the same length.

Among marsupials, the large macropods have the longest periods of maternal care for the young, which are called joeys. Grey kangaroo joeys remain in the pouch for between 284 and 300 days. It's not uncommon to see a mother kangaroo or wallaby with a large, half-grown joey poking a head or foot or both out of her stretchy pouch. The large kangaroos are the

This wallaby's joey may be ready to start exploring the world beyond the pouch.

The big muscles in kangaroos' hind legs propel them forward in a motion that scientists call saltation—a bouncy, bounding leap.

only marsupial species in which a mother may give birth to a new offspring while a partly grown one is still nursing. These large macropods have two nipples inside their pouches, so that a mother can nurse a newborn and an older youngster.

Kangaroos and wallabies are grazers that feed on grass and leaves. While grazing they typically walk about slowly on "all fives," resting their tails and forelimbs on the ground as they swing their hind legs forward with each step. They also balance on their tails when they rear up on their hind legs to look around them. At the slightest sign of danger they leap into action, bounding across the plains with the springy hopping gait that astonished the first European visitors. Good-sized kangaroos and wallabies can reach speeds of up to 30 miles an hour (48 km an hour) for short distances, with high-speed jumps of 10 feet (3 m) or so. Some Australians think that nothing is a better image of their homeland than a line of leaping 'roos silhouetted against the evening sun.

Clutching her fur and clinging with their tails as well as their paws, young Virginia opossums climb over their mother. This adaptable species is North America's only marsupial.

C H A P T E R **F O U R**

American Opossums

Have you ever heard of "playing 'possum"? It's what one American marsupial does when it wants a predator to ignore it. That marsupial is the Virginia opossum, *Didelphis virginiana*. When threatened with danger— and occasionally at other times as well—the opossum enters a state that scientists call catatonia. The animal lies as still as if it were dead, sometimes with its mouth open, usually with its body and tail curled.

Why does the opossum pretend to be dead? One explanation is that it "plays 'possum" to confuse predators, but a more likely reason is to avoid fighting with another opossum. Opossums have been known to remain in a catatonic state for as long as six hours. Most of the time, though, the opossum returns to "life" after a few minutes, when the danger has passed or it senses a chance to escape.

The Virginia opossum has a long, pointed muzzle, a hairless tail, and shaggy gray and white fur. Found across most of the United States and north to Ontario, Canada, it is a familiar evening or nighttime visitor to many suburban neighborhoods. It is also seen, all too often, along the sides of roads and highways, killed by automobile traffic. Although some people regard the opossum as a pest or "varmint," it's good to remember

With its scaly tail curled around its snout, an opossum can fake death for hours. At any moment, though, it may start moving again as though nothing has happened.

that this hardy creature is the only marsupial that managed to make its way north across the Central American land bridge, and the only marsupial that has lived in North America for the past 15 million years or so. It belongs to the largest suborder of American marsupials.

OPOSSUMS

The American opossums form the suborder Didelphimorphia, which contains about sixty-six species. One opossum from this suborder—no one knows exactly which species it was—became the first marsupial ever seen in Europe. In 1500 it was carried from Brazil to Spain, where it was shown to Queen Isabella. The opossum happened to be a female with young. Seeing how carefully the opossum tended and defended her off-spring, carrying them everywhere, the queen declared that the animal was a wonderful mother.

The family of mouse opossums contains about 53 species of small, long-tailed marsupials. They range in total length from 4.5 to 27.5 inches (11.5 to 70 cm). Usually about half of that length is tail. Mouse opossums are found from Mexico to southern Argentina, near the tip of South America. These marsupials lack pouches. Instead, their mammary glands are inside

Most marsupials have one to three babies at a time, but an opossum usually gives birth to half a dozen or more tiny young. Although she can nurse up to a dozen infants in her pouch, it is rare for that many to survive.

Found throughout Central America, the Mexican mouse opossum nests under logs, in dense thickets, or in burrows. By night it creeps around the forest floor, eating insects and fruit.

grooves or folds in the skin of their stomachs. Newborns tuck themselves into these grooves and cling to their mother's nipples.

The mouse opossum family includes fruit-eaters, insect-eaters, and some species that prey on birds' eggs and small lizards. A few species have evolved to live in fairly harsh conditions high up in the Andes Mountains of South America. One species of short-tailed mouse opossum, *Monodelphis domestica*, lives in Brazil, Bolivia, and Paraguay. It sometimes moves into people's houses. It is a welcome addition to households because it kills insects, rodents, and stinging scorpions.

The southernmost American marsupial is a mouse opossum called the Patagonian opossum, *Lestodelphys halli*. A carnivore that feeds on mice and small birds, the Patagonian opossum has been known to eat half its body weight in a single night. Like some other American and Australian marsupials, *L. halli* has a tail that can store fat to serve as a backup food source.

Another family of American marsupials includes the lively, arboreal woolly opossums, which have striped faces and prehensile tails. The woolly opossums use their tails both for climbing and for carrying things. Also in this family is the single species of black-shouldered opossum, *Caluromysiops irrupta*. Native to the Amazon rain forest, the black-shouldered opossum is a slow-moving marsupial that moves from tree to tree and feeds on nectar. It spends most of its time high in the forest canopy and seldom comes down to earth.

Also found in the Amazon is the bushy-tailed opossum, *Gved Gironia venusta*. Scientists have not yet learned much about this species, which is known

The bare-tailed woolly opossum lives in the South American rainforest and is almost never seen on the ground. A nimble arboreal acrobat, this marsupial grips branches with its prehensile tail.

Two white spots above the eyes give the four-eyed opossum its name. These marsupials are good climbers and sometimes build basketball-sized nests of leaves in tree branches.

only from a few specimens. They think that it is arboreal and may be a hunter of insects.

The family of pouched opossums includes the Virginia opossum and seven other species. Two of these species belong to the genus *Philander.* They are called four-eyed opossums because white spots above their eyes look like a second pair of eyes. These small, slender marsupials with naked tails and ears live in wet areas and feed on freshwater animals such as crayfish and snails, as well as insects, earthworms, eggs, and fruit. They build large round nests in low trees or bushes.

The thick-tailed opossum, *Lutreolina crassicaudata,* has plushy fur and a long, lean body that reminds some people of a mink or weasel. It lives in grasslands and is an omnivore, feeding on just about anything it can find or catch. Thick-tailed opossums have diverse tastes in housing, too. Some live in holes in trees, others build nests of grass and reeds, and still others move into empty burrows made by other animals, such as armadillos.

The world's only semi-aquatic marsupial is the yapok or water opossum, *Chironectes minimus.* About the size of a large domestic cat, the yapok has webbed hind feet, water-repellent fur, and a pouch that can be tightly closed with a muscle to keep it waterproof, while holding a pocket of air for the young inside. The yapok swims and dives in freshwater streams

A yapok prepares to take to the water on Barro Colorado Island, a nature preserve in the Panama Canal.

and lakes, hunting for crayfish, shrimps, and fish. Its range stretches from southern Mexico through Central America to northern Argentina.

SHREW OPOSSUMS

The second suborder of American marsupials is the Paucituberuclata. This suborder contains seven species of small marsupials called shrew opossums. They got their name because they resemble shrews, tiny carnivorous placental mammals.

The shrew opossums have long heads, small eyes, sharp teeth, and stiff, short fur. All seven species are found only in South America. They live in dense, humid vegetation in the foothills of the Andes Mountains and travel along tunnel-like runways through thick brush and grass. Two species of shrew opossums have been found only near Chiloe Island, Chile, and are believed to be rare.

A Mystery Marsupial

The monito del monte measures about 8 inches (20 cm) from the tip of its pointed nose to the tip of its furry tail. Its soft, silky fur is brown and grayish white, except for rings of black fur around its large eyes. These rings give the monito del monte the look of a mouse that is surprised to find itself wearing eye makeup.

The monito del monte lives in South America, in the cool, moist forests of southern Chile. It likes thickets of Chilean bamboo and uses that plant's waterproof leaves, along with twigs, to build nests on branches or on the ground under logs. The monito del monte eats worms, insects, and tiny lizards but has been known to enjoy apples in captivity. Called colo-colo by the local Indian people, the monito del monte is thought by some to be a sign of bad luck. People have been known to burn down their houses just because a monito del monte was seen scurrying about inside. To taxonomists, though, this small, shy animal is a question mark.

The monito del monte is a marsupial. Its scientific name is *Dromiciops gliroides,* and it is the only species in its genus, its family, and its suborder, the Microbiotheria. Even though *Dromiciops* lives in South America, scientists are divided over whether it is more closely related to the American marsupials (the Ameridelphia) or to the Australian marsupials (the Australidelphia). The monito del monte has some features in common with each group. To make things even more confusing, it has a few features—especially the arrangement of its teeth—that are found in placental mammals but not in other marsupials.

Some scientists think that *Dromiciops* is the last survivor of a group of marsupials that evolved in South America and later gave rise to the Australidelphia. They have suggested the name Gondwanadelphia for this group. Others think that *Dromiciops* may be a remnant of a line that branched off from the marsupial family tree before the rest of the surviving suborders evolved. If that is true, the monito del monte is a living fragment of a very ancient stage in the history of mammals. Sadly, the loss of the monito del monte's habitat in recent years has made its numbers drop. The World Conservation Union (IUCN), which monitors the status of plant and animal species around the world, has given *Dromiciops* another classification. They have labeled the species vulnerable, which means that it is at risk of becoming threatened.

The monito del monte ("monkey of the mountain") may be a living fossil, an evolutionary link to some of the earliest marsupials.

What does the future hold for the Tasmanian devil? This tough little marsupial faces many threats, including a deadly, mysterious disease.

Living with Marsupials

During the 1990s wildlife photographers and biologists in Tasmania saw, to their horror, that something was terribly wrong with the Tasmanian devils. A vicious form of cancer was attacking their faces and killing them. Called devil facial tumor disease (DFTD), the rapidly growing threat was having a severe effect on the island's devils. By 2003, some devil populations had dropped by 85 percent. Yet no one knew what was causing the disease, whether it had happened to devils before, or whether it was contagious and able to spread from one devil to another. Some observers suspected that DFTD had been triggered by environmental pollutants such as agricultural pesticide or chemicals sprayed on roads to control dust.

In December 2006 the Tasmanian government reported that devil sightings in the northeastern part of the state, where DFTD was first seen, had dropped by 90 percent over the previous ten years. The total number of sightings across the island was down by 41 percent. The possibility that the Tasmanian devil could disappear like the Tasmanian wolf suddenly seemed very real.

The western third of Tasmania appeared to be free of DFTD, although experts feared that the disease could not be prevented from spreading to that region as well. Although scientists have not yet identified the cause of DFTD, they are becoming fairly certain that it is contagious. Government agencies that deal with wildlife and the environment are working to prevent the disease from spreading to healthy populations of devils, to breed a captive population of healthy devils, to monitor the progress of the disease in the wild, and to organize research into the cause of DFTD and possible treatments.

No one knows what the future of the Tasmanian devil will be. In addition to the devastating effects of a fast-acting, mysterious disease, devils are still killed—illegally—by some people who regard them as pests. They are also threatened by non-native animals, such as foxes, that humans have introduced to Tasmania. Finally, the loss of wild habitat to ranching and other human uses has broken up the island's once-large population of devils into many small, isolated populations. Some of these groups may be weakened or damaged by inbreeding.

DFTD is a frightening and extreme danger, but the overall range of threats to the Tasmanian devils is typical of the problems faced by many other marsupial species today, in both Australia and the Americas.

HAZARDS TO MARSUPIALS

The World Conservation Union (IUCN) is an international association of wildlife and conservation organizations. It tracks the status of plant and animal species worldwide and keeps a Red List of those in peril. In 2006, the IUCN listed 79 marsupial species in seven suborders as vulnerable, endangered, or critically endangered. In other words, nearly a third of all marsupials were in trouble.

Scientists who have studied the history of wildlife know that species rise and fall over time. Extinction is part of the natural order of things. But in modern times, when a large number of modern species are suddenly in trouble, the trouble is often rooted in human activity.

Kangaroos appear in many Aboriginal rock paintings. Modern researchers have found that Aborigines possess a wealth of knowledge about marsupials and their habits.

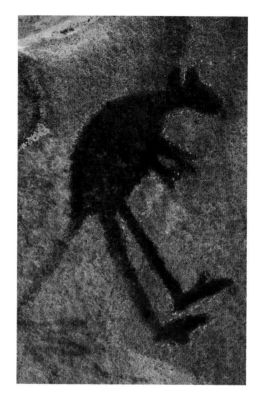

People have lived with marsupials for thousands of years. Kangaroos, wallabies, and other marsupials have long held an important place in the art and mythology of the Aborigines of Australia, for example. The Aborigines hunted these animals for food and skins, and they were knowledgeable about the biology and ways of life of many species. For example, the Adnyamathanha people, who live in the southern Australian mountains known as the Flinders Ranges, favored red kangaroos for eating, but they preferred possum skins for making bags to carry their possessions. The skins of yellow-footed rock wallabies, the Aborigines found, were ideal for carrying water.

No one knows for certain whether hunting by the Aborigines led to the extinction of the giant marsupial species of the Pleistocene, such as the 10-foot (3-m) kangaroos and wombats twice as large as those seen today. Some researchers who have studied the history and lifestyle of the Aborigines think that while their activities may have driven some species into extinction, the native people lived in balance with many other species. The same cannot be said, however, for modern human societies.

The three biggest human-caused threats to marsupials are extermination, introduced species, and habitat loss. Extermination is simply the wiping out of a species. It is what happened, for example, when people hunted the Tasmanian tiger into extinction. People have also tried to wipe out Australian marsupials to free grazing land for livestock. Between 1877 and 1930, more than 27 million medium-sized marsupials were killed in the Australian state of Queensland alone under government Marsupial Destruction Acts.

Marsupials may also be destroyed as pests when they eat farmers' crops. Sometimes farmers kill animals, like the Virginia opossum, simply because the animals seem to be a nuisance. Because they have been known to raid chicken roosts and to rummage through garbage cans, opossums are often considered useless and troublesome creatures. Wombats have been hunted in Australia not because the animals themselves are pests but because of their burrows. Ranchers don't like the fact that sheep can break their legs when they stumble in a burrow. Even more worrisome, wombat

Opossums make an important contribution to ecosystem health by scavenging dead animals and by eating such pests as locusts and slugs.

Matschie's tree kangaroo is native to a small part of New Guinea, where wild populations are endangered by hunting and habitat destruction. Several zoos around the world have started captive breeding programs in the hope of saving the species from extinction.

burrows can become havens for rabbits, which have become a severe pest problem since they were introduced to Australia.

In some places, people continue to hunt wallabies, kangaroos, and opossums for food. Some marsupials have also been hunted for their skins in modern times. Given the widespread public love of koalas today, it's hard to imagine that they were once slaughtered for their soft, warm fur, but it's true. In 1924 alone more than 2 million koala skins were exported from Australia.

The foxes that compete with Tasmanian devils for habitat and resources (and sometimes eat devil young) show what can happen when people introduce animal species to new environments. Dogs, cats, rats, and other introduced species have upset the ecological balance in many marsupial environments, usually with bad results for the marsupials.

Habitat loss, in the end, may pose the greatest threat to endangered marsupials. Large-scale logging in New Guinea and tropical South America puts several dozen species of bandicoots, tree kangaroos, and opossums at risk. In Australia, the ongoing loss of dry forest and brushland could threaten many of the smaller marsupials, such as possums, "mice," and quolls.

Do Tigers Still Roam Tasmania?

The last time a wild Tasmanian tiger is known to have been killed was in 1930. The last known surviving member of the species *Thylacinus cynocephalus* lived in a zoo in Hobart, Tasmania. It died there in 1936. The records of Hobart's city council mention the death of the tiger, with a suggestion that the city should try to obtain a new one for the zoo.

No new Tasmanian tiger was ever found. The tiger—or Tasmanian wolf, or thylacine, as some people call it—had been wiped out. In the future, the only way people could see Tasmanian tigers would be to look at the stuffed or preserved specimens in museum collections.

After fifty years had passed without evidence of a living thylacine, the Tasmanian government declared the species extinct. But was it really extinct? Some people in Tasmania and elsewhere think that a few tiny populations of tigers still exist, living in remote parts of the Tasmanian wilderness.

Over the years, there have been as many as a thousand reports that someone has sighted a tiger, or has found footprints that might be those of a tiger. Some reports of sightings even place the tiger in Victoria, on mainland Australia. As of early 2007, however, no one had produced evidence—such as photographs, videos, hair, or body wastes—that could be tested. At least nine major, well-organized scientific searches for thylacines in Tasmania have come up empty. As one conservation biologist in the Tasmanian government said in 2005, "There are plenty of people who think they've seen a thylacine. Whether they have or not is a different issue." Every year, dozens of believers trek into Tasmania's forested valleys, hoping to see and document the fabled tiger. Others simply cherish the hope that this amazing animal has, against all odds, survived into the twenty-first century.

THE FUTURE OF MARSUPIALS

Australia's northern hairy-nosed wombat, *Lasiorhinus krefftii*, may be the world's most endangered marsupial. It might even be the world's most endangered mammal. The World Conservation Union considers the northern hairy-nosed wombat critically endangered. In early 2007, Australia's Department of the Environment and Water Resources described the species as endangered and likely to become extinct if threats continue.

Northern hairy-nosed wombats once lived in several parts of the states of Queensland and New South Wales. As ranching spread across Australia, the wombats found themselves competing for food with cattle and sheep. Buffel grass, a type of grass introduced to feed livestock, is not part of the wombat's diet since the wombats eat native grasses. But after buffel grass took over many grazing areas, wombats had fewer food sources and had to travel farther to reach them. In addition, the non-native rabbits were also competing with wombats for food and territory. All of these stresses caused the population of northern hairy-nosed wombats to plummet. The last known population of these animals is a small group that lives in a forest in central Queensland.

In 1971, Epping Forest National Park was created to protect the wombats and their habitat. About a decade later, cattle were removed from the park. Later still, a fence was built to keep the wombat habitat safe from dingoes, which prey on wombats and their young. Since that time, the number of northern hairy-nosed wombats has slowly risen from its all-time low of about 30 animals.

By 2000 park managers estimated that 113 northern hairy-nosed wombats lived in the park. Only 25 of them, though, were females of breeding age. Wildlife conservation officials are working to preserve this remnant population of northern hairy-nosed wombats by safeguarding their habitat and perhaps through a captive breeding program to increase their numbers. The future of the species, though, is uncertain. Do enough females

Wearing a portable pouch, a zoo biologist serves as a foster parent to an eight-month-old orphaned wallaby.

survive to create a healthy population, free of the genetic dangers of inbreeding? And if the wombats' numbers increase, will there be safe habitats for them in the wild?

Perhaps people will be motivated to protect and preserve marsupials once more is known about the ecology of these creatures—how they interact with their environments. Scientists are just beginning to understand the ways that marsupials affect the world around them. Take the bettongs, short-nosed rat-kangaroos in Australia. They dig for food and to build burrows, and some of their burrows are quite large. Soil studies have shown that these burrows help plant life in the area by reducing erosion and by breaking up the hard soil so that it can absorb rain. Many other species of marsupials are known to spread seeds and pollen, contributing to the growth of new trees and other plants. In their interactions with other creatures and with their physical environments, marsupials may fill ecological roles that are not yet known.

Like the northern hairy-nosed wombats, many of the most seriously threatened marsupials are now protected by conservation and environmental laws in their countries. Australia and other nations where marsupials live have created wildlife or habitat preserves that offer a refuge to marsupials as well as many other species. Will these measures be enough to save the endangered marsupials? There is hope for large, beloved species such as koalas and Tasmanian devils, "superstar" marsupials that have captured the public imagination. With luck, the small, shy, and secretive marsupials—quolls, possums, shrew opossums, gliders, and their relatives—will also make their way into the future.

With the help of people who care about wildlife and the environment, marsupials such as these wallabies will have brighter prospects for the future.

adapt—To change or develop in ways that aid survival in the environment.

altricial—Born in a relatively helpless state; requiring lengthy parental care.

anatomy—The physical structure of an organism.

ancestral—Having to do with lines of descent or earlier forms.

arboreal—Tree-dwelling.

carnivore—An animal that eats meat.

conservation—Action or movement aimed at protecting and preserving wildlife or its habitat.

convergent evolution—Process in which two groups of animals evolved separately but have similar features because they are adapted to similar habitats or ways of life.

crepuscular—Active at dawn or in the evening.

diurnal—Active in the daytime.

eutherian—Placental, or having to do with mammals that nurture their unborn young in the uterus with the help of an organ called a placenta.

evolution—The pattern of change in life forms over time, as new species, or types of plants and animals, develop from old ones.

evolve—To change over time.

extinct—No longer existing; died out.

genetic—Having to do with genes, material made of DNA inside the cells of living organisms. Genes carry information about inherited characteristics from parents to offspring and determine the form of each organism.

herbivore—An animal that eats plants or parts of plants, such as fruits and seeds.

incubate—To keep eggs or young animals at the proper temperature for development.

insectivore—An animal that eats insects.

marsupial—A mammal whose young are born tiny and undeveloped, then spend an extended period nursing. Many marsupials carry their nursing young in a special pouch on the outside of the mother's body.

metatherian—Another name for a marsupial.

nectar—Sugary liquid produced inside many flowers.

nocturnal—Active in the nighttime.

organism—Any living thing.

paleontology—The study of ancient life, mainly through fossils.

pesticide—Something that kills organisms that humans regard as pests.

placental—Refers to mammals that nurture their unborn young in the uterus with the help of an organ called a placenta.

taxonomy—The scientific system for classifying living things, grouping them in categories according to similarities and differences, and naming them.

terrestrial—Living on the ground.

vertebrate—An animal with a backbone.

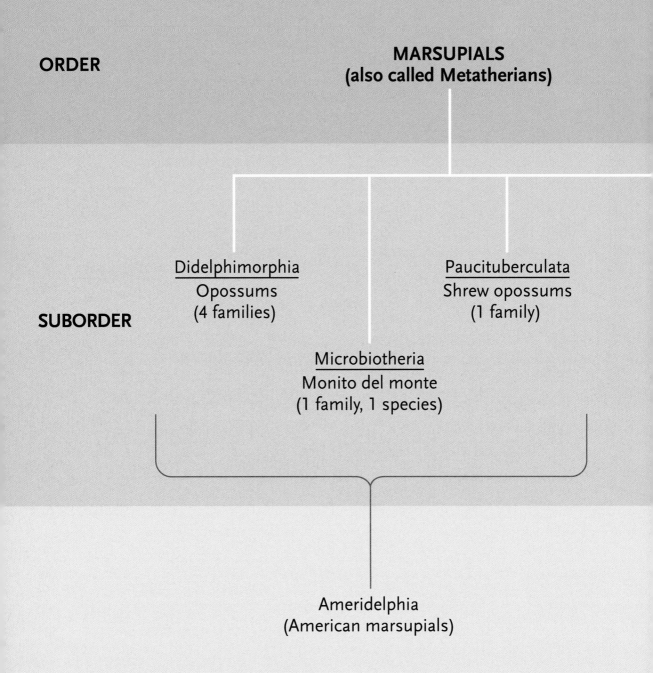

MARSUPIAL

ORDER

MARSUPIALS
(also called Metatherians)

SUBORDER

Didelphimorphia
Opossums
(4 families)

Paucituberculata
Shrew opossums
(1 family)

Microbiotheria
Monito del monte
(1 family, 1 species)

Ameridelphia
(American marsupials)

FAMILY TREE

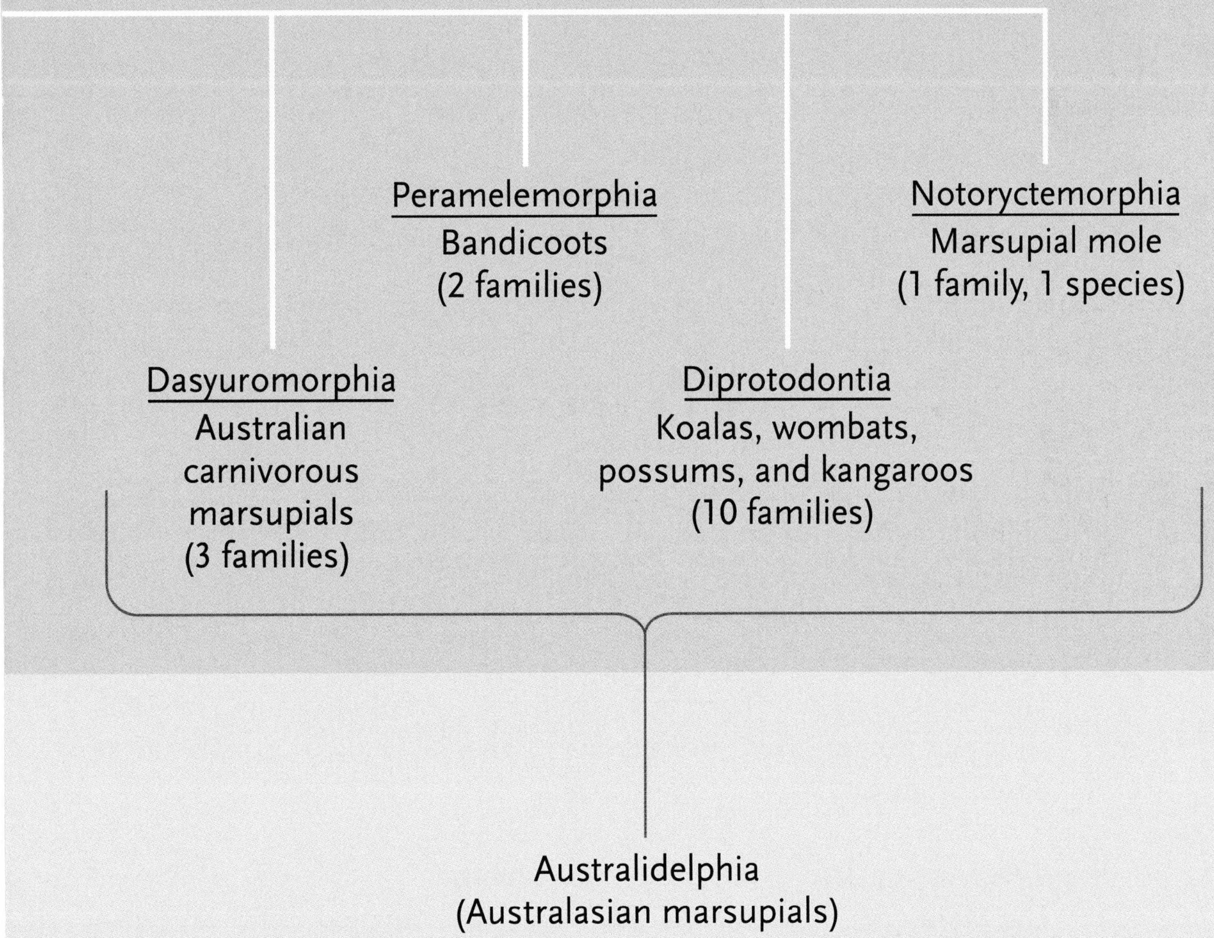

Peramelemorphia
Bandicoots
(2 families)

Notoryctemorphia
Marsupial mole
(1 family, 1 species)

Dasyuromorphia
Australian
carnivorous
marsupials
(3 families)

Diprotodontia
Koalas, wombats,
possums, and kangaroos
(10 families)

Australidelphia
(Australasian marsupials)

The author found these sources very helpful when researching this book.

Armati, Patricia, Chris R. Dickman, and Ian D. Hume, editors. *Marsupials.* Cambridge, UK: Cambridge University Press, 2006.

Dawson, Terence J. *Kangaroos: Biology of the Largest Marsupials.* Ithaca, NY: Cornell University Press, 1995.

Domico, Terry. *Kangaroos: The Marvelous Mob.* New York: Facts On File, 1993.

Graves, Jennifer A. M., Rory M. Hope, and Desmond W. Cooper, editors. *Mammals from Pouches and Eggs: Genetics, Breeding and Evolution of Marsupials and Monotremes.* Melbourne, Australia: CSIRO, 1990.

Jones, Menna, Chris R. Dickman, and Mike Archer, editors. *Predators with Pouches: The Biology of Carnivorous Marsupials.* Melbourne, Australia: CSIRO, 2003.

Nowak, Ronald M. *Walker's Marsupials of the World.* Baltimore, Johns Hopkins University Press, 2005.

Owen, David and David Pemberton. *Tasmanian Devil: A Unique and Threatened Animal.* Crows Nest, Australia: Allen & Unwin, 2005.

Owen, David. *Thylacine: The Tragic Tale of the Tasmanian Tiger.* Crows Nest, Australia: Allen & Unwin, 2003.

Triggs, Barbara. *The Wombat: Common Wombats in Australia.* Sydney, Australia: University of New South Wales Press, 1996.

Tyndale-Biscoe, Hugh. *The Life of Marsupials.* Revised. Melbourne, Australia: CSIRO, 2005.

Woodford, James. *The Secret Life of Wombats.* Melbourne, Australia: Text Publishing, 2001.

I N D E X

Page numbers in **boldface** are illustrations.

A B O U T   T H E   A U T H O R

Rebecca Stefoff is the author of a number of books on scientific subjects for young readers. She has explored the world of plants and animals in Marshall Cavendish's Living Things series and in several volumes of the AnimalWays series, also published by Marshall Cavendish. For the Family Trees series, she has authored books on primates, flowering plants, amphibians, birds, marsupials, and fungi. Stefoff has also written about evolution in *Charles Darwin and the Evolution Revolution* (Oxford University Press, 1996), and she appeared in the *A&E Biography* program on Darwin and his work. Stefoff lives in Portland, Oregon. You can learn more about her and her books at www.rebeccastefoff.com.